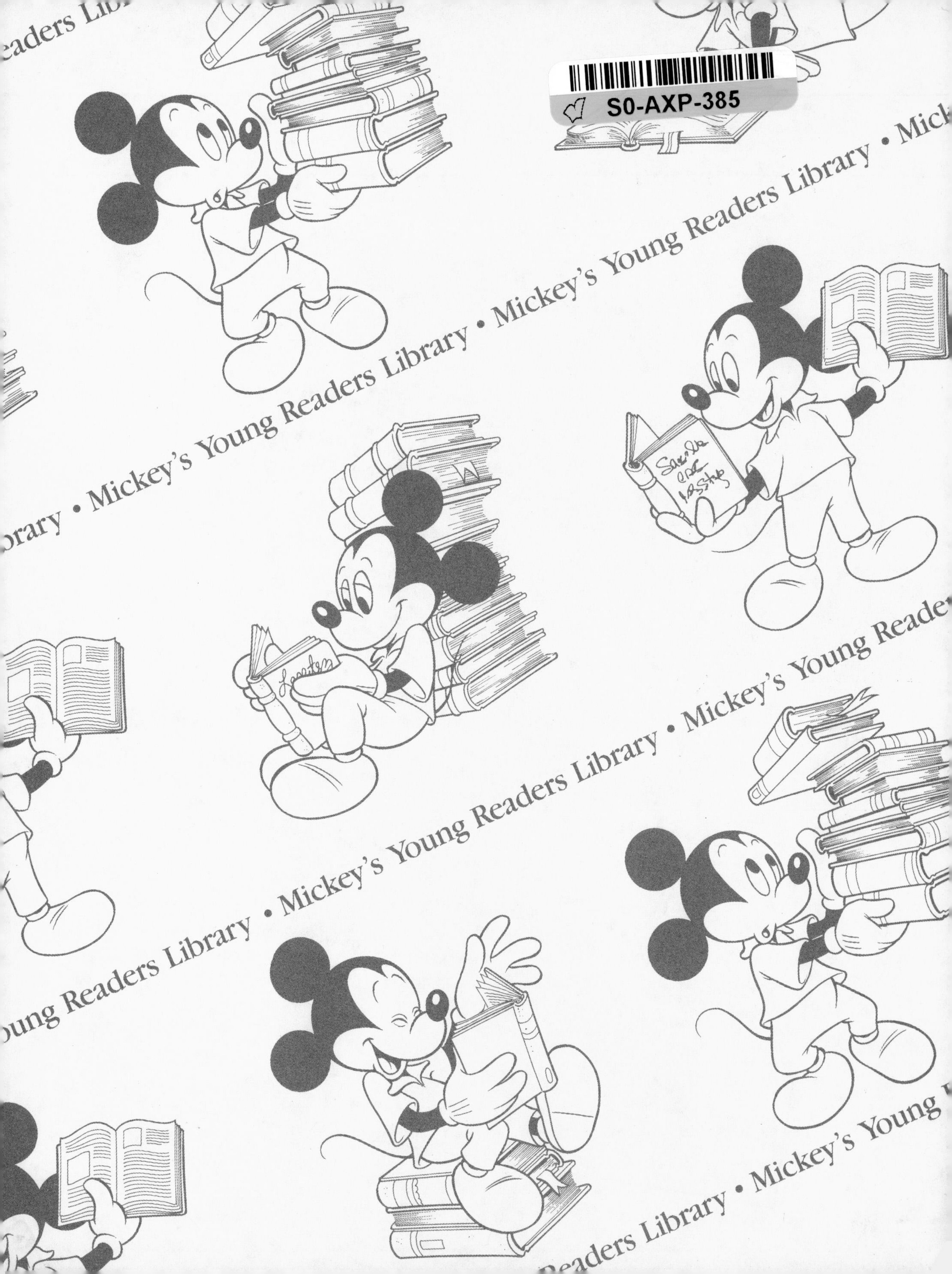
Mickey's Young Readers Library

A Letter to Parents from the Publisher

Mickey's Young Readers Library

Dear Parent,

Learning to read and *loving* to read don't always go hand in hand. To solve this dilemma, The Walt Disney Company has produced MICKEY'S YOUNG READERS LIBRARY. This series has been especially designed by educational experts to give your young reader a positive early reading experience.

The stories are modern adaptations of those familiar children's classics (fairy tales, folk tales, Aesop's fables) that have charmed young readers for generations. And every book features favorite Disney characters.

MICKEY'S YOUNG READERS LIBRARY contains three very special elements:

1. *Simple activities at the end of each story*, carefully created to develop comprehension and reinforce the controlled vocabulary used in every book;
2. *Word Fun—Volume 18*, a full-color activity book designed to build vocabulary AND develop critical-reading skills;
3. *Young Readers Guide—Volume 19*, a book brimming with high-interest games, activities, and projects for you to do with your young reader. All of these suggestions reinforce comprehension skills and expand the vocabulary featured throughout the entire series.

Join the MICKEY'S YOUNG READERS LIBRARY program—and watch your child begin a lifetime of successful reading.

Very truly yours,

Jodie Satterfield

Jodie Satterfield
Publisher

Mickey's Young Readers Library

VOLUME
19
Young Readers Guide

© MCMXC **The Walt Disney Company.**
Developed by The Walt Disney Company in conjunction with Nancy Hall, Inc.
Written by Tina Thoburn, Ph.D.
This book may not be reproduced or transmitted in any form or by any means.
ISBN 1-885222-52-1
Advance Publishers Inc., P.O. Box 2607, Winter Park, FL. 32790
Printed in the United States of America
0987654321

Mickey's
Young Readers Library

An early introduction to a lifetime of
READING EXCELLENCE

A Guide To Better Reading

The *Young Readers Guide* is designed to help children increase their reading power. It briefly summarizes each book in MICKEY'S YOUNG READERS LIBRARY and provides suggestions to help children understand and enjoy the stories, while expanding their vocabularies.

In addition, the guide identifies the classic children's stories that have been used as a basis for these newly created adventures. Many of the activity ideas demonstrate ways for children to make sense of the timeless values taught in these folk tales, fairy tales, and Aesop's fables and ways to incorporate them into their daily lives.

Suggestions for Using the Books

The *Young Readers Guide* contains a special spread devoted to each of volumes 1 through 18 in MICKEY'S YOUNG READERS LIBRARY. Each book spread includes the following:

Illustration and Moral: The cover of each volume is pictured in full color with one of the favorite storybook characters and the moral of the story.

Book Description: This section provides a brief summary of the adapted story and indicates the classic literary selection on which the story is based.

Improving Your Child's Reading: This section includes suggestions for improving your child's comprehension of what he or she has read. It also provides ideas for building a good reading and writing vocabulary.

Increasing Understanding provides a variety of ways for your child to get more meaning from the text, as well as from the pictures. The suggested activities include, for example, having your child retell the story in his or her own words, act out the story, and draw pictures of major story events.

There are also ideas to help your child interpret the underlying moral of each story. After you and your child discuss what the character has learned by the end of the book, the activities will help your child examine and clarify his or her own values as well.

Once you see how successful the techniques in this section are, you will want to adapt them to discuss books other than those specifically recommended.

Building Word Wisdom includes suggestions for understanding important words in the story, focusing on particular word groups:

> words used for names (nouns)
> words used for actions (verbs)
> words used to describe other
>   words (adjectives)
> words for numbers
> words for colors
> words that describe positions in space
> words that describe size
> words for food
> words with opposite meanings
>   (antonyms)
> words for bicycle parts
> words that describe winter
> words that describe sounds
> words that begin with the same sound
> words for tools
> prefixes (parts that change word
>   meanings)
> words that express feelings

Some of the suggestions show children how to use phonic clues to decode words. Others help them develop classification skills, an important thinking skill to sharpen critical-reading abilities. All of the suggestions will improve your child's reading performance (in school and at home), laying the foundation for a lifetime of successful reading habits.

Fun for Young Readers This section is chock-full of games, activities, and field-trip ideas to help you and your child go beyond the book to use real-world experiences to promote a greater understanding of the vocabulary words featured in each story. In this section are directions for art projects, writing projects, planning a birthday party, visiting interesting places, and many, many more exciting things for you and your child to do together and for your child to do independently.

Answers to Activity Pages This section provides answers for the four activities con-tained in the back of every storybook. The answers are listed by individual activity under the headings *Think About It* and *Fun With Words.*

A Special Word About Volume 18, Word Fun (An Activity Book for Young Readers): This volume is a unique feature of the MICKEY'S YOUNG READERS LIBRARY series. This book contains a wealth of games and activities to help expand your child's reading, writing, and speaking vocabulary. At the end of this volume are ways to use this activity book and ideas for going beyond the activities featured in *Word Fun* to further expand your child's vocabulary.

Do's and Don'ts for Better Reading

It is never too early to create a nurturing atmo-sphere to develop your child's reading power. Here are some positive ways to motivate and support your child in these important growing years, and a few cautions, too.

Read Together as a Family The hundreds of research studies conducted to deter-mine those factors that affect reading success universally support the two common-sense notions that "the more a young child's family reads, the more that child will desire to read" and "the more opportunities young children have to read, the better they learn to read." Thus, you have in your hands the means to make your child want to read, and the means to help your child learn to read well! Just pro-vide lots of frequent occasions to read to and with your child. Sometimes you should both read silently; at other times you might take turns reading to each other.

Provide Many Things to Read In addi-tion to the books in MICKEY'S YOUNG READERS LIBRARY, make sure your young-ster has plenty of other reading materials. These materials need not be expensive, but they should be about subjects that interest your child. Encourage your child to browse through your newspapers, catalogs, and magazines, and let him or her cut out words from old issues to make up stories. You may want to subscribe to magazines published especially for children. And don't forget the fun of reading cookbooks together in order to choose favorite foods to cook together.

Use Your Local Library It's a proud day when a youngster gets his or her own library card! Visit the local library with your child so he or she can pick out new books to read. And watch for special free library programs where your child can hear the librarian read stories aloud, join a reading club, see movies based on books or about authors, or participate in art projects related to favorite children's books.

Respect Your Child's Reading Choices Most parents want their children to read uplifting materials, books that are "good" for them.

Sometimes, however, young children don't find their parents' choices very interesting, and would prefer to read materials less desirable from the parents' point of view. This is a time for compromise. Whenever possible, your child will read more books, read longer, and read with more enjoyment if he or she has a lot of say in what is read. So let your child choose most of his or her own reading material. By frequently allowing your child to choose independently, you can slip in a choice of your own now and then without unpleasant confrontations.

Talk About What Your Child Has Read One of the main ways you can help your child develop good reading comprehension skills is to discuss the material your child has read. Ask factual questions about what happened in the story, when it happened, where it happened, who did it, and so on. Also ask interpretive questions about why it happened, what the characters were thinking, and what may happen next. Encourage your child to retell the whole story to see if he or she remembers the sequence of events, and to act out important parts to emphasize how the characters influenced the outcome of the story.

Play Word Games An invaluable aid to the young reader is helping him or her develop a good vocabulary. Understanding the meanings of words, how they relate to each other, and how they are used is critical to understanding the content of written material. That is why this series provides vocabulary and comprehension activities at the back of each story, as well as an entire volume (Volume 18) devoted to vocabulary-building activities.

Encourage Your Child to Write Reading teachers have discovered in recent years that writing can be an invaluable aid to reading, and vice versa. Provide lots of writing paper and writing implements—pencils, pens, crayons, markers, and so on. Encourage your child to retell the stories in MICKEY'S YOUNG READERS LIBRARY in his or her own words, or to write original stories. (Don't worry too much about the spelling at first; instead, concentrate on helping your child get ideas on paper. Grad-

ually you can help make your children aware that others can read their stories more easily if they use standard spelling.) Children will also enjoy illustrating these stories and binding the best of them into books for their friends to read.

Don't Make Reading a Chore This is an important caution. Try to make reading time an enjoyable time for both you and your child. It is better to have several short, pleasant sessions than one prolonged, tiring session. And always try to end on a high note, so your child will be eager to start the next story time together. Successful end-of-session activities include telling each other the favorite part of what you read, drawing pictures, having a reading-time snack, or giving each other a great big "Isn't it fun to read together?" hug.

Don't Demand Perfection When you are reading together, be forgiving when your child makes mistakes or doesn't know a word. Treat each session as a new, fun-learning experience. Correct your child gently, helping him or her decode the word. If a word is not easily sounded out, just say the word yourself and have your child repeat it. You may want to write the word on a small card, and then have your child trace over it and, if possible, illustrate it. Go back over the "hard parts" at a later time, and praise your child for any gains in reading power.

Don't Make Your Child "Perform" Many children enjoy reading in a sheltered situation, yet are intimidated by having to read to strangers, or even to other members of the family. Ask your child whether he or she would like to read aloud to others before announcing that he or she will do so. If a "performance" will be expected by a visiting grandparent, for instance, practice together well in advance of the visit. And let your child choose a favorite easy story for the occasion.

Using the stories in the MICKEY'S YOUNG READERS LIBRARY series in conjunction with the ideas and activities in this guide is a surefire way to ensure that your child not only learns to read, but learns to love reading as well.

Mickey's Birthday Surprise

ALL THAT GLITTERS ISN'T GOLD!

Mickey's Young Readers Library

VOLUME 1

Mickey's Birthday Surprise

A WALT DISNEY BOOK FOR YOUNG READERS

Mickey's Birthday Surprise is a modern adaptation of *The Nightingale*, a fairy tale by Hans Christian Andersen. Mickey, enchanted by a mechanical kitten that he receives for his birthday, doesn't notice that his pet kitten feels ignored. When Mickey's pet kitten disappears and he rescues her from danger, they both realize how much she really means to Mickey.

Improving Your Child's Reading

INCREASING UNDERSTANDING

Drawing Pictures   Discuss the story with your child. Help your child choose several major events in the story to illustrate. Then ask him or her to arrange the pictures in the correct sequence. After stapling the pages together, allow your child to read his or her version of the story to you.

The Moral of the Story   Ask your child to tell you what he or she has learned from the story. Discuss how each character felt about the mechanical kitten. Point out that Mickey learned that the novelty of a new toy or a new friend sometimes distracts a person from thinking about the feelings of another whose presence is taken for granted.

BUILDING WORD WISDOM

Words That Describe Feelings   Many words that describe feelings are used in *Mickey's Birthday Surprise*. When reading the story with your child, stop when reaching a word that describes a feeling. Ask your child to tell about a time when he or she felt that way. Share an experience of your own as well.

FUN FOR YOUNG READERS

Plan a Birthday Party   Help your child plan a birthday party for a friend. Decide whether or not it will be a surprise party; choose a date; and plan whom to invite, what games to play, and what food to serve. About two weeks before the party, help your child make and mail invitations. Shop together for food and a birthday present. Your child should share in the responsibility of decorating the house, wrapping the gift, and cleaning up after the party.

Book of Faces   Leaf through several newspapers and magazines with your child and select several pictures to paste in a booklet. Discuss each picture with your child. How does the person in the picture seem to feel? Why does your child think so? Help label each picture with a word that describes how the person in the picture feels.

Make Me Happy   Play a game of "Make Me Happy" with your child. One player is sad and must wear a deep frown. The other player can tell jokes or do whatever it takes to make the first player smile. Once the frown turns into a smile, players trade places and play again.

"Feelings" Pendants   Make several "feelings" pendants with your child. First cut out circles of cardboard. Then have your child color in an appropriate face on each. Label the faces and punch a hole in the top of each. Then thread an 18-inch piece of string or yarn through the hole in each circle and knot both ends to make a necklace. Your child may want to wear and change the necklaces to express changing feelings.

ANSWERS TO ACTIVITY PAGES

THINK ABOUT IT

How Did They Feel?   1. Mickey liked the toy kitten very much.   2. Pluto thought the toy kitten was nice, but he would rather have played with his ball.   3. Molly was scared by the toy kitten.   4. Mickey still liked the toy kitten, but realized that Molly was more important.

True Feelings   1. F   2. T   3. F   4. T   5. F

FUN WITH WORDS

Act How You Feel   Answers will vary.

Birthday Wordmaking   Some words are:
one-letter words: a, I   *two-letter words:* at, is, it, up
three-letter words: ate, are, bat, eat, hat, ire, pat, rat, sat, bay, day, hay, pay, ray, say, bed, bet, her, pet, red, set, dip, hip, his, pie, rib, rip, sip, the, tip, bit, hit, pit, sit, pub, rub, tub, sup
four-letter words: bait, bare, bear, bier, burp, dare, date, dear, diet, hare, hate, hear, hers, hire, pare, pear, pets, pier, pure, rare, rate, read, sire, step, sure, they, this, tire
five-letter words: birth, heart, pussy, share, stare

Donald's Big News

Don't jump to conclusions before you're sure of the facts!

Donald's Big News is a modern adaptation
of a classic fairy tale, *Chicken Little*. Donald overhears
Grandma Duck and incorrectly assumes that
Grandma's conversation about her lost recipe is a discussion
about losing her farm. After rousing the whole
town of Duckburg to help Grandma, Donald learns
not to jump to conclusions before learning all the facts.

Improving Your Child's Reading

INCREASING UNDERSTANDING

Retelling the Story   Having your child repeat the story in his or her own words will reinforce understanding of the story. Your child may feel comfortable repeating the story to a favorite doll or pet. Listen in on the retelling, and ask pertinent questions if the story seems to get "off track."

The Moral of the Story   Help your child learn to look at the deeper meaning of the story by asking him or her to tell you what Donald learned. Older children may be asked to give the moral of the story in one sentence. Point out that it is often unwise to spread information before you are sure of all the facts.

BUILDING WORD WISDOM

Nouns   After your child has read or listened to the story several times, ask him or her to think about all the items that were brought to the yard sale. Point out that a word that names a person, place, or thing is called a *noun*. Leaf casually through the book with your child and ask him or her to point to pictures of things that are nouns. Have your child find the word for each noun in the story. Point occasionally to a verb or adjective and ask if that word is a noun. Have your child make a list of his or her favorite nouns.

FUN FOR YOUNG READERS

Your Own Yard Sale   Help your child plan and prepare for a yard sale. Go through the house and make a list of all the items that are no longer needed or used by the family. Discuss what day(s) and hour(s) to hold the yard sale. Where will it be? How will you tell people about the sale? (Signs, advertisements in the town paper, flyers, and so on.) What supplies will you need to have on hand? How much will each yard-sale item cost? What will you do with the items that aren't sold?

Visit a Yard Sale   Look through the newspaper with your child for advertisements for yard sales. Select one to attend. At the sale, discuss the price of the items for sale with your child.

Note how the table(s) are set up and the items displayed. Are a lot of people attending the sale? Talk to the person in charge. Is business "good" or "not so good"? What could be done to make the sale better?

Gossip   The next time several of your child's friends are over to play, introduce them to the game of "Gossip." Have the children sit in a circle on the floor. One child starts by whispering something in the next child's ear, such as "Mary has red hair." This is repeated, whispering from one child to the next, all around the circle. It can only be whispered once between each pair of children. The last child repeats what he or she has heard (or thinks he or she has heard). Compare this with the original statement. Discuss how rumors might get distorted by the same method of repetition even among well-meaning people.

ANSWERS TO ACTIVITY PAGES

THINK ABOUT IT

The Main Idea   Sentence #2. #1 is just a good way to get rid of things you don't want or to make some extra money. #3 is also a good rule to follow, but Donald did not have Grandma's recipe. #2 describes what happened in the story, and the lesson Donald learned.

Match It Up   1. banner—Gyro Gearloose   2. pies—Daisy   3. games and toys—Huey, Dewey, and Louie   4. wad of bills—Scrooge   5. hammock and pillow—Gus Goose

FUN WITH WORDS

Your Yard Sale   Answers will vary.

What Did Grandma Lose?   The correct path is: wagon with toys; yard-sale banner; hammock, quilt, and pillow; pies; wad of bills; Grandma's recipe.

Minnie's Giant Plan

Minnie's Giant Plan is a modern
adaptation of an Irish folk tale, *A Woman's Wit.*
Minnie saves Elmo, the friendly local giant, from Igor, the
out-of-town bully, by dressing up Elmo as a giant baby. When
Igor discovers that the giant he has come to fight has
a baby the size of Elmo, he leaves town in a big hurry. Minnie's
plan shows that if you use your head, you don't need to
be physically strong to win the battle.

Improving Your Child's Reading

INCREASING UNDERSTANDING

Answering Questions A good way to help your child's understanding of the story is to ask questions as you read. Pause occasionally and have him or her tell you what has just happened in the story. If necessary, review parts of the story with your child to refresh his or her memory.

The Moral of the Story To help your child learn to think beyond the events of the story, discuss how the events showed that a clever plan worked better than a physical battle to beat a mighty opponent. Ask your child what he or she would have done in a similar situation. Assist your child in applying the moral of this story to a real-life situation where he or she may have used a physical solution to a problem when a clever plan would have worked better.

BUILDING WORD WISDOM

Words for Size After your child has become familiar with the story, discuss the fact that there are many different words that describe the sizes of people and things. Ask him or her to point out several of these words for size. Then, say one of the words and have your child point out an object in the room of corresponding size.

FUN FOR YOUNG READERS

Visit a Museum Children are fascinated by dinosaurs because of their great size and ferocity. If possible, arrange a visit to a local museum with a dinosaur exhibit. Point out that even though many dinosaurs are "big," they too, like the giants Elmo and Igor, come in different sizes. Ask your child to compare the sizes of the dinosaurs using the size words found in the story.

Draw a Giant Picture Tape several pieces of paper together and ask your child to draw a figure to fill the whole space. Then have your child draw a similar figure on a smaller sheet of paper. Let your child compare the pictures, telling you what things are different and what things are the same in each.

Comparing Sizes Collect several bottles or boxes of varying sizes and shapes. Ask your child to arrange them in order of size, from largest to smallest. For verification of the size order, bottles may be "tested" by filling the smallest bottle with water. Then have your child pour it from one bottle to the next, adding water to fill each time. Discuss the difference between "tallest," "widest," and "largest" as labels for the containers.

ANSWERS TO ACTIVITY PAGES

THINK ABOUT IT

Reading Faces 1. Minnie is thoughtful because she's trying to come up with a plan. 2. Igor is scared because he believes that Elmo is larger than he originally thought. 3. Elmo is happy because Igor was scared away.

What's Wrong With This Picture? 1. Picture on the wall is upside down. 2. Igor is sitting in a chair that is too small for him. 3. The pair of scissors that Minnie is holding is too large. 4. The suit Minnie is making for Elmo is too small.

FUN WITH WORDS

Matching Sizes 1. Minnie is the shortest. 2. Elmo and Igor are larger than Minnie. 3. Minnie is smaller than Elmo. 4. Igor is the largest. 5. The smallest chair and coat belong to Minnie; the middle-sized chair and coat belong to Elmo; the largest chair and coat belong to Igor.

A-Maze-in' Minnie The correct path is: the bolt of cloth; the spool of thread; pair of scissors; thimble; sewing basket; sewing needle; Elmo's house.

How Pooh Got His Honey

It's impossible to please all the people all the time!

How Pooh Got His Honey is a modern adaptation of an Aesop fable, *The Miller, His Son, and the Donkey*. When Pooh runs out of honey, he decides to ask Christopher Robin for a refill. However, before he does, Gopher, Tigger, Owl, and Rabbit each advise Pooh on how he should get his honey. Pooh listens to every one, trying to please them all. Unfortunately, he ends up with no honey and disastrous results at every turn. Finally Pooh learns that when you try to please everyone, you end up pleasing no one— not even yourself.

Improving Your Child's Reading

INCREASING UNDERSTANDING

Retelling the Story   Help your child retell the story in his or her own words. Refer to a few pages that illustrate important events to help your child tell the story in correct sequence. You may also provide key words as clues.

The Moral of the Story   To help your child learn to "read between the lines," discuss the hidden lesson of the story. What was Pooh's original plan to refill his honey pot? How did he eventually get it filled? Point out that when Pooh tried to please everybody else, he ended up with no honey. His original solution was, in fact, the best one of all.

BUILDING WORD WISDOM

Positional Terms   After your child has become familiar with the story, read it aloud once more. This time, pause when you come to a positional term, such as "up," "down," "over," "below," and so on. Ask your child to supply the missing word.

FUN FOR YOUNG READERS

I Spy   Play a simple game of "I Spy" with your child. The rule for this game is that you must use a positional term. For example, you say "I spy something red *under* the table." Then your child names that object. (If you describe objects in relation to yourself or your child, try to remain in the same spot for the entire game.)

Honey Recipes   Leaf through a cookbook with your child. Together, select a recipe that contains honey. Try making the recipe with your child and, if appropriate, invite friends or other family members to sample it.

Make-a-Word Game   Help your child make letter cards by writing each letter of the alphabet on an index card. (Make three cards for each vowel.) Place the cards face down on a table and mix them well. Take turns drawing five cards from the pile (or until each player has at least one vowel). Once you draw all of your cards, make as many words as you can, on that turn, using the cards in your hand. Score

one point for each word. Return the cards to the pile and mix well after each turn. The first person to get 25 points wins the game.

Other Stories   Read other stories to your child. Ask your child to raise his or her hand every time he or she hears a positional word. If your child doesn't recognize the word, simply repeat the sentence, stressing the word in question.

ANSWERS TO ACTIVITY PAGES

THINK ABOUT IT

Pooh's Friends   Clockwise from upper right: 1. Tigger   2. Owl   3. Christopher Robin   4. Rabbit   5. Roo (at left) and Piglet (at right)   6. Gopher

What's the Story?   1. Pooh's honey pot was empty.   2. Pooh tried digging, bouncing, flying, and picking flowers.   3. Pooh got honey by asking Christopher Robin.   4. He learned not to worry about what others thought, and to have confidence in his own ideas.

FUN WITH WORDS

Up, Down, and All Around   1. Pooh   2. Roo   3. The bee at the right by the hole.   4. The bee at the left by the hole.   5. Honey tree   6. Pooh   7. Roo   8. Pooh   9. Bird   10. Pooh

Honey-Pot Word Search

Scrooge and the Golden Eggs

Scrooge and the Golden Eggs is a modern adaptation of an Aesop fable, *The Goose and the Golden Eggs*.
Driven by his greed, Scrooge tries many ways to make an ordinary goose lay golden eggs. When the goose flies away, leaving him with less than he had when he began, Scrooge learns that greed doesn't pay.

Improving Your Child's Reading

INCREASING UNDERSTANDING

Body Language Says It All   To help your child learn to pay attention to story details, ask him or her to act out the story as you read. Read slowly and pause often, especially when two or more characters are involved. Suggest that your child assume the different postures and facial expressions of the characters as he or she acts it out.

The Moral of the Story   Ask your child to tell you what Scrooge learned in the story. Point out that Scrooge was so anxious to purchase the goose and become still wealthier, that he did not stop to think about whether or not a real goose could lay golden eggs. Also discuss how his greed made him treat the goose so badly that she wanted to escape. In the end, Scrooge's greed blinded him to the reality of the situation, and he ended up with nothing, not even the goose!

BUILDING WORD WISDOM

Adjectives   Point out several words on the first few pages of the story that are used to describe other words. These adjectives include *bright, beautiful, golden,* and *special.* Point out to your child that these words are used to describe other words in the story (*bright* describes day, *beautiful* describes goose, and so on). Read through the story again together. Have your child point out other adjectives.

FUN FOR YOUNG READERS

Decorating Eggs   Have your child help you shop for eggs, noting the different prices, sizes, and packaging. Hard-boil the eggs to prepare them for easy decorating. Decorate the eggs with crayons or paints; glue on small pieces of ribbon and paper; or dye them. It might be fun to decorate different eggs with a crayon portrait or a glued–on snapshot of a member of the household.

Further Reading   Your child may enjoy reading *Jack and the Beanstalk,* a classic fairy tale, to learn about another goose that lays golden eggs.

Learn About Eggs   Visit a farm, a children's zoo, or even the library, to learn more about eggs. What sizes are the different eggs? Which animals lay eggs? What is the most common egg? The rarest? Many museums now have examples of dinosaur eggs, which fascinate young children. What colors are the different eggs? Which egg is the largest? The smallest? At home, your child might like to make a booklet of drawings of the different eggs he or she has learned about.

The Birds   Visit your local library to learn more about the way various birds nest their eggs. Where do the birds build their nests? What do they eat? How big are they? What do they have in common, and what is different about them? See if your child can identify some of the common birds in your neighborhood.

ANSWERS TO ACTIVITY PAGES

THINK ABOUT IT

Tell the Story   1. Scrooge buys the goose.   2. Scrooge calls Grandma Duck for advice.   3. Scrooge tries to show the goose what to do.   4. The goose flies away.

Act It Out   Your child should use facial features and body actions to show the following physical conditions: 1. extreme heat 2. extreme cold 3. being very sleepy   4. being confused and upset.

FUN WITH WORDS

Which Goes With What?   1. soup/hot 2. tree/large 3. horn/loud 4. snowman/cold 5. pillow/soft

Wordmaking   Some words include: *two-letter words:* do, go, no, so, or   *three-letter words:* den, doe, dog, eel, egg, end, gee, leg, led, log, old, see   *four-letter words:* dole, gold, legs, lend, send, sole

Mickey's Magic Bottle

Mickey's Magic Bottle is an updated version of the well-known fairy tale *The Three Wishes*. After Mickey asks Donald and Goofy to take care of his magic bottle in his absence, Donald and Goofy conjure up the genie in the bottle, who gives them three wishes. Both Donald and Goofy wish before they think, and they end up learning to be careful what they wish for —because it just might come true!

Improving Your Child's Reading

INCREASING UNDERSTANDING

Causes and Consequences   Help your child learn to listen carefully by encouraging him or her to retell the story in his or her own words. If questions arise, review the relevant portions of the story. You might help your child along by asking questions such as, "What happened next? Why?" "What did Donald do next?" and so on.

The Moral of the Story   Ask your child to tell you the lesson that Donald and Goofy learned in *Mickey's Magic Bottle*. Explain that they didn't think about what they said before they said it, and as a result, they made some pretty silly wishes. They got just what they asked for, but not what they wanted. Ask your child to tell about some situations where he or she said something silly and instantly regretted it.

BUILDING WORD WISDOM

Prefixes dis- and un-   Review the concept of opposites with your child. Remind him or her that words such as *hot* and *cold* mean the opposite of each other. Ask your child to give you an opposite for *unhappy*. Point out that to make the opposite of *happy*, we simply add the prefix *un-* to the front of the word. To make the opposite of *appear*, we add the prefix *dis-*, making the word *disappear*. Mention that both prefixes mean "not"—not happy and not appearing. When your child reads, have him or her watch for other words that use the un- and dis- prefixes.

FUN FOR YOUNG READERS

Wish Book   Help your child make a wish book. Staple several pieces of paper together to form a booklet. Your child may fill the pages with cut-out pictures of things for which he or she would like to wish. Then suggest that your child make another booklet showing things he or she might wish to give other people. Each picture can be labeled with the recipient's name.

Make Believe and Reality   Discuss the difference between make believe and reality with your child. Have him or her name some things that are real and some that are make believe. Discuss cartoon shows, regular programs, and news from television. Go through storybooks and have your child tell you which things are real and which are make believe.

Using Your Imagination   Ask your child to draw a picture of some make-believe character (good or bad) and describe what the character is like.

ANSWERS TO ACTIVITY PAGES

THINK ABOUT IT

What Comes Next?   1. Picture of Donald and Goofy with the bottle and the genie.   2. Picture of Goofy with a table full of food.   3. Picture of Goofy with the drumstick stuck to his nose.

Make-a-Wish   Donald wanted to wish for cars, houses, and money.

FUN WITH WORDS

Match-a-Word   1. a   2. b   3. d   4. c

The Genie's Message   made/unmade; appear/disappear; happiest/unhappiest

Donald's Dream

Don't put off till tomorrow what you can do today!

Mickey's Young Readers Library · VOLUME 7

Donald's Dream

A WALT DISNEY BOOK FOR YOUNG READERS

Donald's Dream is a modern adaptation of Washington Irving's story of *Rip Van Winkle*. Donald procrastinates about completing the chores that he promised to do for his friends, and he finds out what happens when he puts off until tomorrow the things that he promised to do today. Luckily for Donald, and for all of his friends, the consequences of his undone chores turn out to be only a dream!

Improving Your Child's Reading

INCREASING UNDERSTANDING

Draw Pictures   To check on your child's understanding of the story, ask him or her to draw pictures of the major events of the story. Then help your child staple the pages together in order so that the story makes sense. Compare your child's book to the original when it is complete.

The Moral of the Story   Discuss the lesson Donald learned from his dream. Point out that he would not have been so overwhelmed by all of the chores if he had done them one at a time, or when he had promised to do them. Letting them pile up made it hard for Donald to do any of them at all. Ask your child to give some examples of times when he or she procrastinated too long. Add a few examples of your own, too.

BUILDING WORD WISDOM

Words for Tools   *Donald's Dream* contains several words naming the tools that Donald needed to do all his jobs. Ask your child to leaf through the book to find pictures of these words, and then to locate the words in the text. What are these tools used for? Look for other tool words in other books and stories. Go through your kitchen or workshop together, looking for tools not mentioned in the story.

FUN FOR YOUNG READERS

Consequences   Help your child match the jobs Donald put off to their consequences. It may help to make a list or chart. Discuss what might have happened if Donald had done all the jobs when he promised, instead of putting them off for a later time. Ask your child to tell about some promises he or she made and didn't fulfill. How did it make him or her feel? How did the person to whom the promise was made feel? Add a few of your own unfulfilled promises, too.

Job Chart   Help your child make a chart of his or her jobs around the house. Make a list first, discussing which jobs should be done daily, weekly, and so on. Arrange these in time categories on a large chart or poster. Each job name may be illustrated by your child. You might like to apply a small gold star or other sticker each time the job is done correctly.

Jobs in Your Neighborhood   Visit a store (grocery, clothing, or other small business) where you have arranged a behind-the-scenes tour. What jobs are performed in the store? Discuss what job your child might like in the future (subject to change, of course), and what he or she thinks are the responsibilities that go with that job.

ANSWERS TO ACTIVITY PAGES

THINK ABOUT IT

Dream-a-Story   1. Scrooge   2. Pluto   3. Goofy   4. Daisy   5. Grandma

Donald's Doings   1. planting a garden for Grandma   2. fixing the roof for Daisy   3. bringing bones for Pluto   4. fixing the alarm for Scrooge   5. fixing a bike for Goofy   6. fishing—something just for Donald

FUN WITH WORDS

Fix-It Word Search

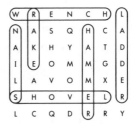

Tool Jumble   1. HRENWC—wrench   2. MMRAHE—hammer   3. SLAIN—nails   4. HOVELS—shovel   5. KREA—rake   6. DDREAL—ladder

Tigger and the Apple Tree

It's best to think before you leap!

Mickey's Young Readers Library

VOLUME 8

Tigger and the Apple Tree

A WALT DISNEY BOOK FOR YOUNG READERS

Tigger and the Apple Tree
is a modern adaptation of *Two Frogs*,
an Aesop fable. Tigger volunteers to help Rabbit
pick the highest apples from the apple tree so that Rabbit
can make applesauce. Tigger ends up bouncing just a bit too
high for his own good. Tigger learns that instead of showing
off how high he could bounce, he should have thought
about how he was going to get down from the tree once
he had bounced up.

Improving Your Child's Reading

INCREASING UNDERSTANDING

Show What Tigger and His Friends Can Do
To help your child learn to pay close attention to the plot and characters of the story, ask him or her to act out the behavior and actions of the characters in the story. If he or she leaves out important details, confuses character traits, or mixes up the order of the story, review the story or parts of it with your child to correct the confusion.

The Moral of the Story Discuss the lesson taught in the story. Point out that Tigger rushed into doing something without thinking about it beforehand. Ask your child to remember times in his or her own life where it would have been wiser to plan his or her actions and think about the consequences before acting. Contribute a few experiences of your own, too.

BUILDING WORD WISDOM

Action Words After your child has read the story several times, point out that a word that describes an action is called a *verb*. Show your child some examples of verbs in the text as you read the story again. After the first few pages, ask your child to stop you when you come to a verb. Do the same thing when you read other stories with your child.

FUN FOR YOUNG READERS

Visit an Orchard or Fruit Stand Plan an outing to a nearby apple orchard or produce market. Ask an employee to explain the different kinds of apples available, their sources and uses. If possible, purchase several kinds and have a "taste test" of your own. Which are sweet? Tart? How many different colors of apples are there? Cut open an apple and two or three other fruits. What is the same about the fruits? What is different? Do they all grow on trees?

Applesauce Recipe Find a recipe for applesauce that contains honey as a sweetener. Your child may enjoy helping you cook and puree the apples into a delicious sauce. If it is practical, allow your child to invite several friends over to sample the resulting applesauce.

The Four Seasons Discuss the four seasons with your child. Have him or her describe what happens during each season. Provide a large piece of paper and drawing or painting materials. Ask your child to draw four pictures of the same apple tree—one for each season. After the drawing is complete, help your child label each season.

ANSWERS TO ACTIVITY PAGES

THINK ABOUT IT

Let's Talk 1. Apple tree 2. Rabbit wanted to make applesauce 3. Pooh, Roo, Tigger, Kanga, Owl, and Eeyore 4. Tigger bounced to reach the apples 5. Tigger learned to be more careful where and when he bounced.

What's Wrong With This Picture? 1. Pooh has an umbrella 2. Pear tree should be an apple tree 3. Roo is in tree 4. Tree is too small

FUN WITH WORDS

What's Going On? 1. Pooh 2. apples 3. Rabbit 4. ground 5. Tigger 6. tree 7. apples 8. apples 9. Tigger 10. basket 11. Rabbit 12. apples

Which Ones Can Do The Same Things? 1. Owl, bee 2. Roo, Pooh 3. Roo, Pooh 4. ball, Tigger

Mickey and the Big Storm

Mickey and the Big Storm
is a modern adaptation of an Aesop fable,
The Ant and the Grasshopper. When Donald and
Goofy hear about a threatening snowstorm, they prepare
to play in the snow, instead of buying food and
supplies. When they become cold and hungry and
have no supplies on hand, they visit Mickey, in the hope
that he is better prepared than they are. Luckily for
Donald and Goofy, Mickey *is* prepared and has more
than enough supplies for himself and his friends.

Improving Your Child's Reading

INCREASING UNDERSTANDING

Stage a Snow Show To help ensure that your child has gathered the correct information about the story, have him or her act out the story for you. Your child may use facial expressions and body movements, along with a running narrative. By providing a few simple costumes and props, this could also be acted out for younger siblings or other relatives.

The Moral of the Story Discuss the lesson that Donald and Goofy learned in the story. How was Mickey's behavior different from theirs? Point out that Mickey gave up a little bit of fun, and so was able to be warm and have food. The motto "Be prepared!" applies to everybody. Ask your child to think about situations in which he or she was unprepared. Share some of your own situations. Discuss what you both might do differently next time.

BUILDING WORD WISDOM

Words for Winter Read through the story again with your child, asking him or her to point out words that describe winter. Help your child make a list of these and other words describing winter. A special list might be made for words or expressions that begin with *snow,* such as *snowman, snowball, snow fort, snow tires,* and so on. You might want to make several lists by category, such as "Things I Wear in Winter," "Things I Do in Winter," "Games I Play in Winter."

FUN FOR YOUNG READERS

Build a Snowman If possible, plan a time when all the family members can get together to build a snowman. Each person should help make up the body of the snowman, and each should contribute something for the snowman to wear.

Being Prepared for a Blizzard Discuss how Goofy and Donald got ready for the storm. Then talk about how Mickey prepared for it.

Discuss the advantages of being prepared for this and other situations. Go through the house together, making a list of items that should be kept in supply at all times. If important items are missing, or in short supply, have your child help you shop for these items.

Winter and Summer Your child might enjoy drawing pictures of the view from a window in your house. Ask him or her to draw one picture of the view in summer and one picture of the view in winter. What is different about the pictures? What is the same? Then have your child draw a picture of him or herself as he or she looks and dresses in the summer and in the winter.

ANSWERS TO ACTIVITY PAGES

THINK ABOUT IT

Getting Snow-Ready Mickey: shovel, firewood, cocoa, food. Donald and Goofy: sled, snowballs, skis, boots, skates.

What Would You Do? Answers will vary.

FUN WITH WORDS

Snow-Word Jumble SNLLBAOWS—SNOWBALLS KISS—SKIS STEAKS—SKATES ANMWONS— SNOWMAN DELS—SLED FKLEANOWS— SNOWFLAKES

Winter Word Search

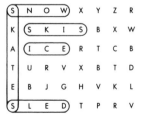

Donald's Magic Stone

THERE'S NOTHING LIKE A GOOD IMAGINATION!

Donald's Magic Stone
is a modern adaptation of the folk tale
Stone Soup. After Donald realizes he has no food
to make dinner, he convinces Goofy to contribute everything
they need for a soup dinner, while all Donald contributes
is his "magic" stone. When the dinner is ready, Donald
feels badly that he has used the idea of a "magic" stone
to fool Goofy. But Goofy lets Donald know that he has been
wise to the "trick" all along, and that he has appreciated
how a little imagination made an ordinary soup dinner into
a whole lot of fun!

Improving Your Child's Reading

INCREASING UNDERSTANDING

Reading Recipe   To check your child's understanding of the story, ask him or her to draw pictures of the items in the story that were used to make the soup. Have your child drop the pictures into a pot, while he or she retells the story in his or her own words, in the proper sequence. Refer to the story if your child gets confused.

The Moral of the Story   Ask your child to tell you what Donald learned in the story. Discuss how Donald admitted the stone was not magic because he was ashamed about tricking Goofy into providing all of the food. Discuss how Donald's imagination almost made the stone really seem magical. Ask your child to tell about a time when he or she used his or her imagination and had a good time as a result. (Be careful to distinguish between using one's imagination and telling a lie.) Tell some stories of your own, too.

BUILDING WORD WISDOM

Food Words   After your child has read the story, ask him or her to think about the different food words used. Ask your child to find the words in the text. You may want to have your child make a food wordbook. Help your child cut out magazine pictures of food. Let him or her paste them onto construction paper, then label the foods. You may want to help your child group similar items (such as fruits, vegetables, meats, dairy products, cereals, and fats). Staple the pages together to make a food wordbook to which your child may refer.

FUN FOR YOUNG READERS

Making Soup   Help your child select a cookbook and look up recipes for soup. Discuss the various kinds of soups found in the cookbook, and imagine how they would taste. Select one recipe that your child would enjoy making. Take your child with you to shop for all the ingredients, and help him or her cook the soup. If possible, arrange for his or her friends to come for lunch so that your child can serve the soup.)

Favorite Recipes   Ask your child to think about all of his or her favorite recipes. Then assist him or her in creating a simple cookbook. For each recipe, help your child list the ingredients, write down the preparation steps, and illustrate the finished product with drawings or cut-out pictures. Staple the recipe pages together and keep them handy for reference when you and your child want to make his or her favorite recipes.

Collecting Rocks   Most children love to collect things, and rocks are easily found in great variety. Help your child start a rock collection by accompanying him or her on a walk around the neighborhood. Small samples may be glued onto a piece of sturdy cardboard for display. Larger samples may be used as decorations in a garden, or as paperweights. Books about rocks may be found in your local library.

ANSWERS TO ACTIVITY PAGES

THINK ABOUT IT

Magic Stone Soup Recipe 1. stone   2. carrots   3. onions   4. flour   5. cabbage   6. potatoes   7. salt and pepper

What Do You Think? 1. No, it was not a magic stone.   2. Donald pretended that the stone was magic because he was hungry and had no food.   3. Goofy.   4. Donald was ashamed because he had tricked Goofy into providing all the food.   5. Goofy might have been fooled for a while, but he caught on to Donald's trick.

FUN WITH WORDS

Soup Words   Answers may vary.

Spell It Out 1. NOOINS/ONIONS 2. RLOFU/FLOUR   3.   REDAB/BREAD   4.   ECHESE/CHEESE 5.   BCABGAE/CABBAGE
6.   ESPOATTO/POTATOES 7.   UTERBT/BUTTER
8.   RROTCAS/CARROTS 9.   ASLT/SALT
10.   VIOLES/OLIVES

Huey, Dewey, and Louie Meet the Witch

Treat people nicely, and they'll treat you nicely, too!

Mickey's Young Readers Library — VOLUME 11

Huey, Dewey, and Louie Meet the Witch

A WALT DISNEY BOOK FOR YOUNG READERS

Huey, Dewey, and Louie Meet the Witch is a modern version of *The Witch*, an old fairy tale. During their search for adventure, the three nephews show great kindness to a bird, horse, and dog who, unbeknownst to the nephews, are under a witch's spell. Huey, Dewey, and Louie then fall into the clutches of this witch, and in their hour of need, the animals they helped, help them in return. By the end of the adventure, the boys and the witch learn the important lesson that if you're nice to others, they'll be nice to you.

Improving Your Child's Reading

INCREASING UNDERSTANDING

Asking "Why?" for Comprehension   One way to help your child learn to pay attention to the content of the story is to ask questions afterwards. Pose questions such as "Why did the nephews feel sorry for the horse?" or "Why did the witch put a spell on the young men?" Allow your child to hold the book while answering the questions, so unknown answers can be looked up if necessary.

The Moral of the Story   Have your child tell you the moral of the story. Point out that the witch was mean to everybody, so everybody treated her meanly. The nephews were kind to the bird, dog, and horse, so the animals were willing to assist the nephews when they really needed help.

BUILDING WORD WISDOM

Words That Begin With the Same Letter or Sound   Many words begin with the same sound. Select one letter or sound at random, and reread the story, having your child stop you when he or she hears another word that begins with that sound. If your child is reading the story with you, select a sound and have him or her stop you when he or she sees another word beginning with the same sound.

FUN FOR YOUNG READERS

The Golden Rule   Discuss the meaning of the golden rule with your child. Point out that "doing unto others as you would have them do unto you" may mean just being polite, but sometimes it means going a little beyond that to help someone else. Have your child tell you about some things that people do that he or she thinks are rude. Has your child ever done these things? How did your child feel when he or she behaved this way? Have your child tell about some things he or she has done for someone else just to be thoughtful. How did this make him or her feel? How did the other person react?

Pack a Suitcase   Point out that the nephews were not prepared for a trip to the forest.

What should they have brought along? Help your child pack a suitcase for an overnight trip. Pack several ways for different destinations—a cold place, a hot place, a wet place. Does your child need to pack food, blankets, and so on? What is different about what is taken for each trip? What is always the same?

A Trip to the Forest   If possible, arrange a time when you and your child can make a trip to a forest or park. Have him or her note the different animals, trees, and other plants found there. Ask him or her to describe what it might be like to spend a night all alone in the forest or park. What sounds would be heard? Who else might be there? Where could food and water be found? What might be seen during the night?

ANSWERS TO ACTIVITY PAGES

THINK ABOUT IT

Helping Hands   The nephews helped the animals in this order: 1. bird 2. horse 3. dog

The Witch's Tale 1. They could not complete the tasks she had set them. She turned them into animals so they would always do her bidding. 2. The witch was angry. She tried to get the bird, dog, and horse to help her. 3. The witch was sad. 4. The witch was very grateful to the nephews. 5. She learned that you should be nice to people if you want them to be nice to you.

FUN WITH WORDS

A Witch-y Message   Do unto others as you would have them do unto you.

A Witch's Brew 1. wand—web 2. bird—beetles 3. horse—hornets 4. dog—dragonfly 5. cottage—caterpillar

Pluto and the Big Race

Pluto and the Big Race
is a modern adaptation of an Aesop
fable, *The Lion and the Mouse*. Morty and Ferdie are
busy building their box car. Mickey and Minnie are busy
getting on with their day. Pluto just wants someone to
play with him, and everyone thinks that all Pluto can do
is to get in everybody's way. But when Morty and Ferdie's
box car disappears, it is Pluto who solves the mystery
and helps them win a box-car race as well! The story
shows that help may, and sometimes does, come from
the least expected places.

Improving Your Child's Reading

INCREASING UNDERSTANDING

Unexpected Endings To make sure that your child understands the story's moral, read the story a second time. Pause frequently to ask questions about the characters and their actions. How did Pluto feel when everyone told him to go away? What happened next? How did Pluto help Morty and Ferdie find their box car? Given the way Pluto was behaving earlier in the story, were you as surprised as Morty and Ferdie that Pluto could be of help? Why or why not? Explain why Pluto turned out to be the perfect character to solve Morty and Ferdie's problem.

The Moral of the Story Ask your child to tell you what Morty and Ferdie learned from Pluto. Point out that you never can tell where help might come from when you need it. Ask your child to tell you about a time when he or she was surprised by help from an unusual or unexpected source.

BUILDING WORD WISDOM

More Action Words Read carefully through the first few pages with your child, pointing out any verbs in the text that describe movement, such as *pushed, sniffed, painted.* From then on, ask your child to find the words related to movement in the text as you read the story together. Help your child make a list of these words. Later, he or she can act out the movements described by the words.

FUN FOR YOUNG READERS

How Did Pluto Feel? Discuss with your child how Pluto felt at the various stages of the story. Ask how your child would feel if the same things happened to him or her. Has he or she ever been guilty of ignoring someone? Has he or she ever felt ignored? Provide some examples of your own experiences as well.

Getting Around Help your child make a poster of the various types of children's transportation. Cut out pictures from magazines, newspapers, and catalogs to paste on a large sheet of paper. Such pictures might include bicycles, tricycles, wagons, scooters, skateboards, roller skates, ice skates, sleds, and so on. Discuss with your child which forms he or she has used, and which he or she would like to try.

Plan a Race Help your child plan a race for friends. This may be a simple footrace, a sack race, or a bicycle race. Have your child decide when the race is to be held, and what will be offered as prizes. (Pencils, crayons, or small gifts may be used for prizes.) If possible, carry through with the plans. Your child might wish to be the judge or to participate in the race.

ANSWERS TO ACTIVITY PAGES

THINK ABOUT IT

Pluto Strikes Again! 1. Minnie 2. Morty and Ferdie 3. Mickey 4. Morty and Ferdie The correct order is (1) Morty and Ferdie with the oil can (2) Mickey, by sleeping on his porch (3) Minnie, because Pluto growled at and frightened a bird in her bushes (4) Morty and Ferdie, because Pluto jumped into their box car

Pluto's Very Bad Day Pluto's day improved when everybody realized that he had something to contribute to the effort, too. (Individual answers will vary)

FUN WITH WORDS

Detective Pluto Follow the path that contains the following words: jumping; sleeping; sitting; running; eating.

What Can Pluto Do? 1. b 2. d 3. a 4. c

Mickey's Little Helpers

One good turn
deserves
another!

Mickey's
Young Readers Library

Mickey's Little Helpers

VOLUME 13

A WALT DISNEY BOOK FOR YOUNG READERS

Mickey's Little Helpers is
a modern adaptation of *The Elves
and the Shoemaker*, a classic fairy tale by the
Brothers Grimm. Morty and Ferdie spend several nights
repairing bicycles for Mickey so that his new bicycle
shop will succeed. Mickey then rewards each nephew
with a special bicycle, demonstrating that
one good turn deserves another.

Improving Your Child's Reading

INCREASING UNDERSTANDING

Be a Reading Detective To make sure that your child has understood the entire story, read through the book again. As you do so, pause at the appropriate pages and ask the following questions: When did he or she know who Mickey's helpers were; when did he or she realize that Mickey knew, too; and does he or she think Mickey was really sleeping at his workbench every time? Ask your child to explain or point to clues in the art that explain his or her answers. If your child seems confused, read over the part of the story in question until he or she draws the correct conclusion.

The Moral of the Story Discuss how Morty and Ferdie helped their Uncle Mickey out of love for him. They wanted his shop to be a success, and they realized he was too tired to repair the bicycles all by himself. Talk about how the boys did not expect anything in return for their good deed—and, in fact, didn't even want Mickey to know that they had helped him. Discuss the concept of doing good deeds for others without expecting to get anything in return. Ask your child how he or she feels when someone does a good deed for him or her.

BUILDING WORD WISDOM

Words Related to Bicycles Most children are familiar with words that describe parts of bicycles. To make a bicycle wordbook, cut out letters from headlines in newspapers and magazines. Help your child use these letters to spell out the words for bicycle parts in the story (pedals, brakes, wheels, and so on). Draw a large, simple bicycle outline and have your child glue the letters to form bicycle words within it.

FUN FOR YOUNG READERS

A Trip to a Bicycle Store Plan a trip to a bicycle store or sports department of a larger store. Look over the bicycles available. What differences are there among them? What sizes are available? In how many colors do they come?

Ask the salesman about who does the bicycle repairs. Does the store sell parts? Compare prices. What equipment makes the bicycles more or less expensive?

Bicycle Safety Discuss the importance of bicycle safety with your child: the do's and don'ts significant to your area. (Do follow the traffic signs; don't ride at night without a light and bright clothing, and so on.) To reinforce the rules, help your child make a poster of the most important bicycle-safety rules.

ANSWERS TO ACTIVITY PAGES

THINK ABOUT IT

Mickey's Mixed-Up Letter 1. We had many customers from the very first moment we opened. 2. We were so busy today that we never even got a chance to sit down.

Do You Remember...? 1. Nobody came to the shop the first day. 2. The customer was entering a race the next day. 3. The nephews worked nights. 4. Mickey pretended to be asleep and saw Morty and Ferdie fixing the bikes. 5. He gave Morty and Ferdie the new bikes they wanted.

FUN WITH WORDS

Bicycle Word Search

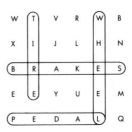

Bicycle Mix-Up 1. helicopter 2. television 3. baseball bat 4. football 5. doll

Scrooge's Silly Day

Don't worry about things that might never even happen!

Scrooge's Silly Day is an updated version of a classic fairy tale, *The Three Sillies*. After working hard to arrange his money neatly, Scrooge worries that the wind will blow it away. An innocent Donald, called in to board up the window, ends up knocking over the neat piles! The only way to decide who will clean up the mess is for Scrooge to find three characters who have worries sillier than his own. At first Scrooge refuses to admit he is being silly, but when he discovers the three silly worriers and compares their worries to his, Scrooge realizes that perhaps he was being silly after all!

Improving Your Child's Reading

INCREASING UNDERSTANDING

Silly Stories/Sensible Readers   To make sure that your child understands the events in the story, as you read through it, ask your child to describe each character's worry.

The Moral of the Story   Ask your child to explain why Scrooge's worry was silly. Point out that, yes, it was possible for the wind to break the window, but the chances of that happening were very slim. Since the window was far stronger than the wind, Scrooge was simply wasting his time worrying about something that probably would never happen when he should have been doing something he enjoyed instead. Discuss how the other three sillies were wasting their time worrying about things that weren't very likely to happen either, and as a result, ended up spoiling the time that they could have spent having fun.

BUILDING WORD WISDOM

Opposites   Tell your child that several pairs of words with opposite meanings can be found in the story (e.g., lucky/unlucky; silly/sensible; neat/messy; happy/sad; worried/calm;). Allow him or her time to look through the book, discovering the various pairs of words. You might wish to write each word on an index card. You may then mix up the cards and take turns matching up the opposite pairs.

FUN FOR YOUNG READERS

Telling Opposites   Play a word-association game (for two or more players). The first player says a word, and the other player must say its opposite. If there are more than two players, play should progress clockwise around the circle.

Silly Drawings   This game may be played with several players. Each player is given four cray-ons and a piece of paper. At the word, "Go," each player begins drawing something (anything will do). After two minutes, everyone stops. Each player passes his or her paper to the person on his or her right, and players then add to the other player's drawing. Continue switching until you receive your paper back. Can you figure out what your drawing has become?

What Is Silly?   Discuss with your child the feeling of being worried. Ask him or her to tell you about the things that worry him or her and why they do. Talk about whether the worries have any real foundation, or if they are just silly worries like Scrooge's.

ANSWERS TO ACTIVITY PAGES

THINK ABOUT IT

Scrooge's Silly Worry   Scrooge worried that the wind would break the window and blow away all his money. He wanted Donald to put boards over the window.

Meet the Sillies   1. Gus worried that if he closed his eyes it would rain and ruin his perfect nap.   2. Gladstone worried that he might run out of good luck.   3. Gyro worried that Earth would spin too fast and that people would get dizzy and be unable to walk.

FUN WITH WORDS

Silly Scramble   1. YEOMN—MONEY
2. ANP—NAP   3. KCUL—LUCK   4. YZZDI—DIZZY
Silly Signs   1. Cows don't fly.   2. Ducks don't give milk.   3. Cars don't fly.   4. Ice cream is not red hot.

Goofy Goes to the Fair

Goofy Goes to the Fair is an adaptation of *The Little Engine That Could™*, a modern classic children's story. At first it seems as if no one can get to the fair—not by train, nor bus, nor truck, nor hot-air balloon. But there is one form of transportation that won't let Goofy and his friends down. Despite the breakdowns, rattling parts, and steep hills that Goofy's car *Old Faithful* faces, Goofy's belief that his car can overcome everything to get him and his friends to the fair pays off. His success proves that if you really believe you can do something, you're bound to succeed.

Improving Your Child's Reading

INCREASING UNDERSTANDING

Remembering Details to Get to the Fair To help your child remember the details and sequence of events in this story, play a movement game similar to "Giant Steps." In order to move closer to the imaginary "fair" on one side of the room, your child has to call out which character he or she is, and which vehicle he or she is in. If correct, he or she may move. If not, he or she stays in place until he or she thinks of the right answer. If necessary, your child may refer to the book to help him or her remember the details.

The Moral of the Story Discuss the lesson about perserverance that the story demonstrates. In spite of every possible thing going wrong with *Old Faithful*, Goofy and his friends would not give up trying to reach their goal. In the end, their faith and belief in Goofy's car (as well as some practical mechanical assistance by Goofy) gets them to the fair!

BUILDING WISDOM

Words for Sounds After your child has become familiar with the story of *Goofy Goes to the Fair*, ask him or her to make the sounds mentioned in the story, at the appropriate times, while you read the story over again. Point out other words for sounds that you and your child may hear during the day. See how your child would spell these sounds. Take turns writing new words for sounds and pronouncing them.

FUN FOR YOUNG READERS

A Trip to a Fair If possible, arrange a trip to a county fair, a farmer's market, or a community festival with your child. Help your child make a list of all the rides available. Be sure to visit the displays of homemade goods, noting the variety of baked goods and sewing samples. What games are being offered? After the visit, ask your child to name his or her favorite events.

Transportation Help your child make a transportation book by pasting magazine pictures of vehicles onto construction paper. Then staple the pages together. As your child finds more pictures of vehicles of interest, he or she can add them to the book.

Visit a Mechanic Arrange a visit to a neighborhood mechanic who is willing to take some time to explain his or her job to your child. Be sure to ask the mechanic about safety.

ANSWERS TO ACTIVITY PAGES

THINK ABOUT IT

Who Went to the Fair? 1. Mickey—train, bus 2. Minnie and Daisy—bus 3. Huey, Dewey, and Louie—farmer's truck 4. Donald—hot-air balloon

Getting to the Fair 1. F 2. T 3. T 4. F 5. T

FUN WITH WORDS

What Sound Does It Make? The horn of *Old Faithful* beeps; the doors rattle; the brakes screech; and on its way to the top of the hill, it coughs.

What's at the Fair?

Mickey and the Troll

VOLUME 16

Mickey's Young Readers Library

Mickey and the Troll

A WALT DISNEY BOOK FOR YOUNG READERS

It's always best to tell the truth!

Mickey and the Troll
is a modern version of the myth *Mercury
and the Woodsman*. Mickey visits a mountain village.
While helping an elderly couple by acting as their shepherd,
Mickey confronts a wicked troll who has caused previous
young shepherds to disappear. When Mickey loses his
wooden shepherd's staff down the troll's well, the troll tries to
trick Mickey into saying that a bronze, silver, or golden
staff is the one Mickey lost. Honest Mickey will not do so,
and the troll disappears in a puff of purple smoke—freeing all
the dishonest shepherds who came before Mickey.
Mickey's honesty showed the other shepherds that honesty
is really the best policy!

Improving Your Child's Reading

INCREASING UNDERSTANDING

Drawing Inferences   To determine how much of the story your child understands and remembers, direct him or her to draw several simple pictures to illustrate answers to the following questions, which are *not* depicted in the story: What had all the shepherds before Mickey done when they met the troll? What did the troll do to those shepherds? What do you think happened when all the shepherds returned to their families? What would have happened to Mickey if he hadn't answered the troll honestly? What would have happened to the elderly couple?

The Moral of the Story   Ask your child to tell you what the story shows us about the right way to behave. Point out that Mickey *might* have gotten rich if he took one of the other staffs, but he knew that the one he had dropped in the well was wooden, and it wasn't honorable to pretend otherwise. Ask your child to share an experience when he or she had to decide whether or not to tell the truth. Share an experience or two of your own as well.

BUILDING WORD WISDOM

Words for Color   Read the story together and have your child point out the various words for colors as they appear. You might visit an art store, where markers, crayons, pencils, and paints come in a great variety of colors. Note the names of the many colors (for example, periwinkle, magenta, and so on), which themselves are very "colorful." While out driving or riding, ask your child to point out the different colors of one type of object (for example, cars, houses, Christmas decorations, and so on).

FUN FOR YOUNG READERS

Visit a Sheep Farm   If possible, arrange a trip to a sheep farm or a petting zoo. Have your child pay special attention to the color and texture of the sheep's wool. The farmer or attendant can explain how the wool is gathered and made into cloth. Look in your local library for books about sheep. Where are they usually raised? What do they eat? Does shearing a sheep hurt it? Why else do people keep sheep?

Make a Sheep   Help your child make some fluffy sheep. Draw an outline of a sheep on a heavy piece of cardboard and cut it out. Paste pieces of cotton wool (or cotton balls) on the body of the sheep. If desired, the sheep may be made into a stick puppet by gluing a clean ice-cream stick or tongue depressor to the back.

Being Honest   For a serious discussion about honesty, find a quiet time when you will not be interrupted. Ask your child to tell you why he or she thinks being honest is important. Point out that telling lies is not only a wrong thing to do, but that other people will learn not to trust you. Reassure your child that even though it may sometimes hurt to tell the truth, it is always the best thing to do.

ANSWERS TO ACTIVITY PAGES

THINK ABOUT IT

A Picture Tale 1. sheep 2. well 3. staff 4. troll 5. troll 6. well 7. troll 8. staff 9. well 10. staff 11. troll 12. staffs

Mickey told the truth about his staff and freed all the young men from the troll's spell.

The True Picture The picture in which Mickey is refusing to take the staff offered by the troll, and the troll appears angry, is the *true picture*.

FUN WITH WORDS

What a Colorful World! green/grass; blue/sky; yellow/sun; white/cloud; purple/mountain; gray/stone wall; brown/tree trunk; red/roses (Answers may vary.)

Where's the H? You cannot hear the *h* sound in the words *hour, honor, herb,* and *honest*.

Donald and the Frog

If you make a promise, you have to keep it!

Mickey's Young Readers Library

Donald and the Frog

VOLUME 17

A WALT DISNEY BOOK FOR YOUNG READERS

Donald and the Frog is a modern adaptation of the fairy tale *The Frog Prince*. During the annual Junior Woodchuck sporting events, Donald Duck expects to win the rowing competition as usual. In the midst of the race, Donald loses his oar. But with the help of a frog to whom he promises his trophy, Donald wins the race. As he proudly accepts the trophy, the frog comes to collect on Donald's promise. Much to the Junior Woodchucks' surprise, a reluctant Donald hands over the trophy, because, as he assures them, a promise once made should not be broken.
To reward Uncle Donald for his sportsmanship, the Junior Woodchucks surprise Donald with another trophy of his own!

Improving Your Child's Reading

INCREASING UNDERSTANDING

A Sporting Story   A good way to help your child learn to pay attention and remember the details in a story is to have him or her perform the story actions as you read the story together. Each time you come to a sporting event, have your child act it out. When you get to the rowing competition, have your child demonstrate Donald's unsportsmanlike and then sportsmanlike behavior. Which activity makes your child feel good about himself or herself? Which one makes him or her feel badly? Ask him or her to explain why.

The Moral of the Story   To help your child learn to think beyond the plot of the story, discuss the lesson we learn about the right way to act. Point out that even though it hurt Donald to give up his trophy, it was the only fair thing to do because he had promised it to the frog, and the frog had completed his part of the bargain.

BUILDING WORD WISDOM

Words for Numbers   After you have read the story several times, ask your child to think about where numbers are used in the story and to find the words used for numbers in the text throughout. To check understanding, have your child show you the correct number of objects for each word. Help your child review these words from time to time to reinforce his or her memory.

Dear Max,

Please come to a picnic in the park on Saturday afternoon from 2 to 4 p.m. Your friend, Kathryn

FUN FOR YOUNG READERS

Picnic in the Park   With your child, plan an outing similar to the one enjoyed by the Junior Woodchucks. Here are some things you can do together:

Writing Invitations   Decide on a time and place for the picnic. Make a list of the friends your child wants to invite. Help your child write and deliver the invitations.

Packing a Lunch   Discuss the menu with your child and have him or her help you make a shopping list. Shop together, and ask your child to help you read the items on the list, crossing them off as you put them in the cart. When you get home, prepare and pack the food together.

Planning the Games   Help your child plan games or contests. For example, you may want to have some simple footraces, play tag, or play hide-and-seek. Also plan some inexpensive prizes for the winners (small boxes of treats, bookmarks, writing pads, crayons, and so on).

ANSWERS TO ACTIVITY PAGES

THINK ABOUT IT

What Happened When?   1. Donald pointing to the lost oar as the frog watches.   2. Donald winning the rowboat race.   3. Donald looking sadly as the frog hops off holding the trophy.   4. Donald holding the trophy overhead.

Be a Good Sport   1. Donald told them that it was more important to be a good sport than it was to win the event.   2. Donald promised to give the frog his winning trophy.   3. At first, Donald was not a very good sport.   4. In the end, Donald did deserve the "Best Sport" award. He realized that he had to keep his promise, since the frog had fulfilled his part of the bargain, and keeping his promise to the frog was more important than taking home the trophy.

FUN WITH WORDS

Number Match   1st = first; 2nd = second; 3rd = third; 4th = fourth; 5th = fifth; 6th = sixth; 7th = seventh; 8th = eighth; 9th = ninth; 10th = tenth.

Words of Sportsmanship   Some of the words are: *two-letter words:* am, an, as, at, hi, in, is, it, on, or, so, to *three-letter words:* ant, arm, art, ash, asp, ham, hat, hap, hip, his, hot, hop, its, man, map, mar, mat, mop, *four-letter words:* ants, arms, hats, hips, hits, hops, mass, mast, mats, miss, mist, mope, moss, most, naps, nits, pans, part, pass, past, pats, pits, port.

Word Fun
An Activity Book for Young Readers

Word Fun (An Activity Book for Young Readers) is chock-full of word puzzles, quizzes, and activities to teach your child the delight and power of words. Helping to expand your child's vocabulary is the best way to improve his or her reading skills. Many of the activities relate directly to word categories featured in the storybooks, but you will also find other new and exciting groupings included for your child to enjoy and explore.

USING MICKEY'S WORD FUN

Your child may do the activities in this book at any time, whether or not he or she has read any or all of the stories in the series.

To begin, read the directions along with your child. You may want to provide a piece of scrap paper on which your child can write the answers, or you may just want to talk about the answers. (Answers are given at the back of *Word Fun*—Volume 18.)

After your child has completed each activity, review the featured words. Talk about how these words go together, and ask your child to think of other words that belong in the same category. Keep using and talking about the words and word categories for several days after you and your child have completed the activities. In fact, most children will enjoy doing the *Word Fun* activities again and again. Follow up with one or more of the word games below, and you'll be surprised how your child's vocabulary will grow.

MICKEY'S FAVORITE WORD GAMES

Guess My Word Agree on a category of words, e.g., "words for colors" or "words that name things in the city." Take turns thinking of a word that fits the category. The person who is IT says, "I'm thinking of a word. Guess what it is." The other players take turns naming a word it might be. The player who guesses the correct word has the next turn to be IT.

Making Word Cards Give your child a pack of three-by-five-inch index cards, or cut out pieces of paper about that size. Also supply a card file, or make one from a small, colorful box. As you work with each new category of words, help your child write one word on each card. If the word can be illustrated, have your child draw a picture to help remember the word. As your child thinks of more words for each category, have him or her add them to the file.

You may also want to provide alphabet divider cards to help your child learn to file the words according to their first letter. Later on, you may help your child learn to arrange the words alphabetically.

Word-Card Concentration Sort out six pairs of cards with words that have something in common. For example, if you are working with synonyms, pick six pairs that have the same meaning (big/large, small/little, happy/glad, angry/mad, thin/skinny, cold/icy). Or you might make six pairs beginning with the same letter (red/round, big/ball, wagon/wish, stone/soup, tub/top, happy/hot). Still another category is rhyming words (sad/glad, cow/how, rake/bake, seeds/weeds, brown/frown, big/pig).

Shuffle the cards and lay them face down in three rows across and four rows down on a flat surface. Players alternate turning up two cards at a time. If the two cards "match," the player keeps both cards and goes again. If the cards do not match, the player turns them face down and the next player goes. The player with the most pairs after all cards have been matched wins the game. The loser gets to begin the next game.

Travel Word Game This is a good game to play while traveling in a car, bus, or train. Look out the window and say, for example, "I see something that rhymes with fat." Your child should look carefully and guess the answer—*hat, cat,* or whatever it is you both have seen. Vary your clues according to the kinds of words familiar to your child. Here are several ideas to get you started:

"I see something that starts with *b*."
"I see something that ends with *t*."
"I see something that is an animal."
"I see something that is orange."

Alphabet Word-Chain Game Take turns naming words that start with consecutive letters of the alphabet. For example, *A* is for *apple, B* is for *boy, C* is for *car, D* is for *Donald, E* is for *elephant,...Z* is for *zebra.* Your child may want to look through *Word Fun* to get help with some of the words.

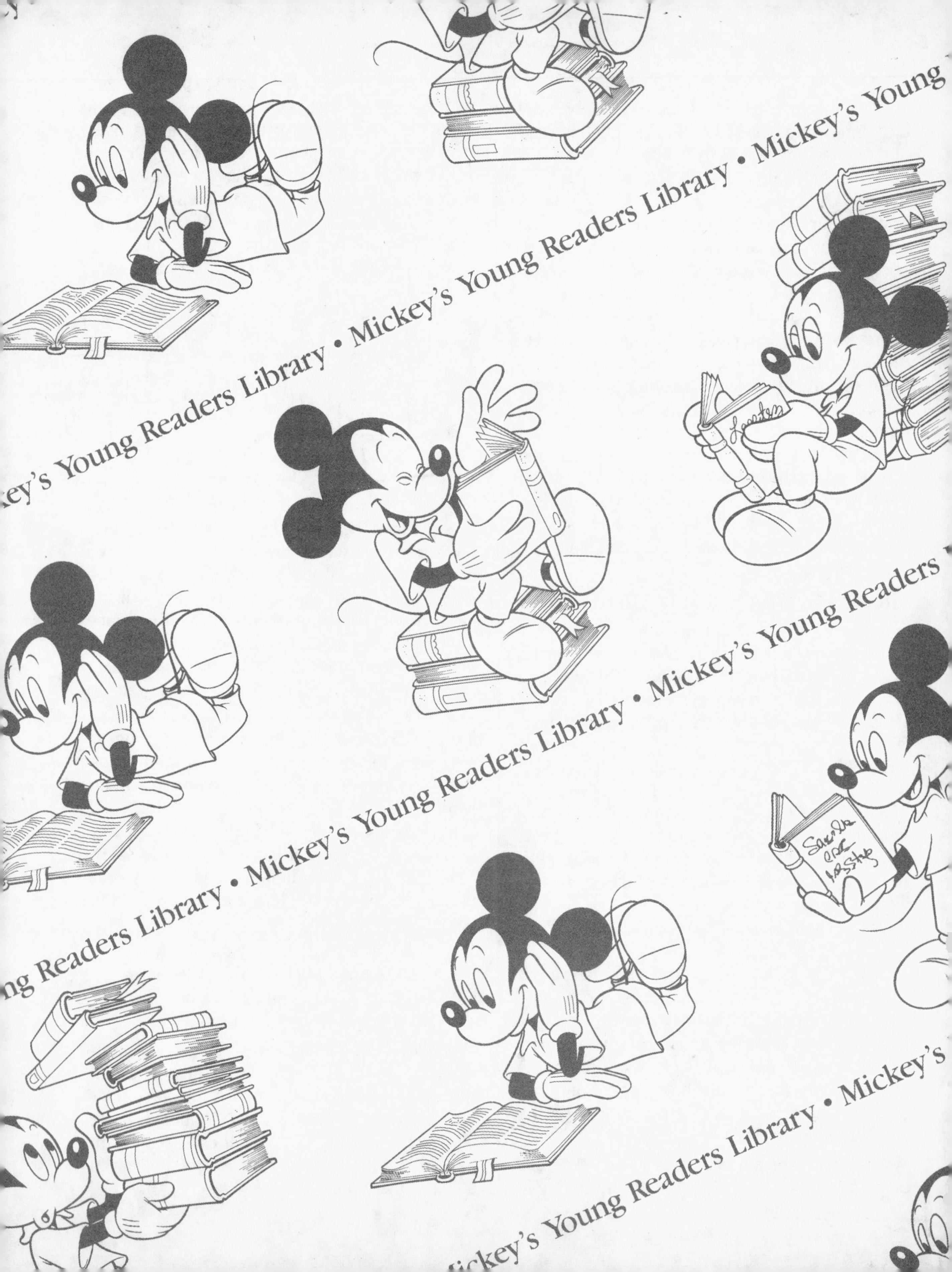
Mickey's Young Readers Library • Mickey's Young